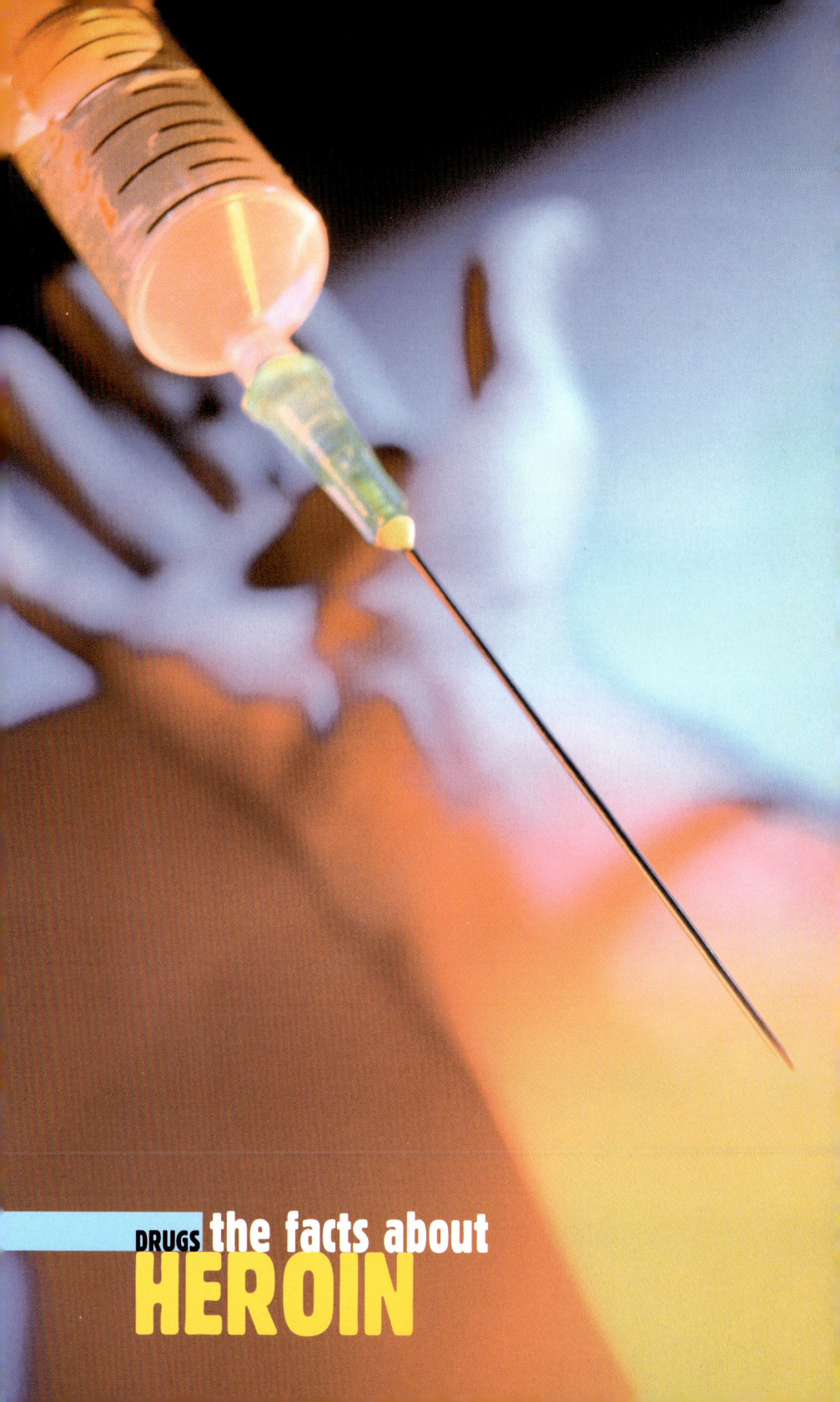

DRUGS the facts about
HEROIN

DRUGS **the facts about**

HEROIN

SUZANNE LEVERT

mc Marshall Cavendish
Benchmark
New York

Marshall Cavendish Benchmark
99 White Plains Road
Tarrytown, New York 10591-9001
www.marshallcavendish.us

Text copyright © 2006 by Marshall Cavendish Corporation

All rights reserved. No part of this book may be reproduced or utilized in any form or by any means electronic or mechanical including photocopying, recording, or by any information storage and retrieval system, without permission from the copyright holders.

All Internet sites were available and accurate when sent to press.

Library of Congress Cataloging-in-Publication Data
LeVert, Suzanne.
The facts about heroin / by Suzanne Levert.
p. cm. – (Drugs)
Summary: "Describes the history, characteristics, legal status, and abuse of the drug heroin"—Provided by publisher.
Includes bibliographical references and index.
ISBN 0-7614-1975-6
1. Heroin habit. I. Title. II. Series: Drugs
HV5822.H4L47 2005
616.86'32—dc22
2005001728

Printed in China
3 5 6 4 2

Photo Research by Joan Meisel
Cover photo: Science Photo Library/Photo Researchers, Inc.

The photographs in this book are used by the courtesy of:
Corbis: Ric Ergenbright, 6; Bettmann, 13, 14; Michael S. Yamashita, 16; Roy Morsch, 21; Lester Lefkowitz, 26; Bojan Brecelj, 44; Gideon Mendel, 46; Tom Wagner/SABA, 74; Tatiana Markow/Sygma, 82. *U.S. Drug Enforcement Administration*: Courtesy www.dea.gov, 18 (top and bottom). *Getty Images*: Andy Bullock/The Image Bank, 40; Frank Micelotta, 55; AFP, 84. *Peter Arnold, Inc.*: Knut Mueller, 64. *Photo Researchers, Inc.*: 1, 2-3, 4-5; National Library of Medicine, 9; Jean-Loup Charmet, 11; A. Pasieka, 29; Jim Dowdalls, 30; Lawrence Migdale, 80.

CONTENTS

1 **The Ultimate High?**   7
2 **What Heroin Does**   27
3 **Dangers of Use and Abuse**   41
4 **The Traffic and the Law**   59
5 **Leaving Heroin Behind**   75

Glossary   88
Further Information   90
Index   92

A FIELD OF OPIUM POPPIES IN PAKISTAN. AFTER POPPIES FLOWER THE PETALS FALL AWAY, EXPOSING AN EGG-SHAPED SEED POD. THE SAP WITHIN THESE PODS IS OPIUM, THE RAW MATERIAL FOR DRUGS LIKE MORPHINE AND HEROIN.

1 Heroin: The Ultimate High?

FOR CENTURIES, man has known about the intoxicating effects of the sap from a flowering plant called the opium poppy, and man has used this sap for good effects and bad. Through a chemical process developed in the 1880s to manufacture a pain-relieving medication, the active ingredient in the sap becomes the illicit drug known as heroin. In addition to acting as a powerful pain reliever, heroin acts to stimulate the pleasure centers of the brain, making it one of the world's most addictive substances.

According to the United Nations International Drug Control Programme (UNDCP), about 9.8 million people around the world use heroin. The U.S.

National Survey on Drug Use and Health, conducted by the Substance Abuse and Mental Health Services Administration in 2003, found that about 3.7 million Americans twelve years of age and older reported using heroin at least once during their lifetimes. That's about 1.6 percent of the population aged twelve years and older in the United States. According to the same survey, about 314,000 people, or 0.1 percent of the total population, reported using heroin in the past year.

Heroin is manufactured from the opium poppy plant, or *Papaver somniferum*. This plant grows naturally in the Middle East, Southeast Asia, and parts of Central and South America. To harvest opium, producers cut the seed pod out of the poppy. The active ingredient in the sap from inside the pod is morphine, which is easily converted to heroin through a simple chemical process. The manufacture and sale, also known as trafficking, of heroin is a multi-billion dollar international business. The cost of heroin use and addiction is even higher in terms of the toll taken on the lives of the men and women, young and old, affected by its use and abuse.

The History of Heroin
Heroin is not a new drug. Indeed, the first known reference to opium is in a Sumerian text from more than 5,000 years ago, in which the plant is called *Hul Gil*, or the joy plant. Throughout history, certain religions have embraced the narcotic effects of the

HIPPOCRATES, THE GREEK PHYSICIAN OFTEN CALLED THE FATHER OF MEDICINE. HIPPOCRATES WROTE ABOUT THE USEFULNESS OF HEROIN AS A PAINKILLER.

poppy plant as a gateway to meditation as well as for pain relief and other medical remedies. Hippocrates, the physician of ancient Greece sometimes called the Father of Medicine, noted the medicinal properties of opium as a styptic, something that can be used to stop bleeding, and as a narcotic, used to treat internal diseases.

Galen, another classical Greek physician well known for his writings on the medical arts, noted how opium apparently "resists poison and venomous bites, cures chronic headache, vertigo, deafness, epilepsy, apoplexy, dimness of sight, loss of voice, asthma, coughs of all kinds, spitting of blood, tightness of breath, colic, the iliac poison, jaundice, hardness of the spleen stone, urinary complaints, fever, dropsies, leprosies, the trouble to which women are subject, melancholy, and all pestilences." While it is true that opium and its derivatives help to relieve pain, coughing, and other conditions, they are far from the miracle drugs touted by these early physicians.

Not surprisingly, the news of opium's special qualities spread, especially when Alexander the Great introduced opium to the people of Persia and India, where poppies grew. By 400 CE, Arab traders were selling opium to China, which would become a leading importer of the drug for centuries.

The Early Opium Trade

By the late 1400s, opium use had spread throughout Asia, the Middle East, and into Europe. Opium dens, where people went to smoke the drug, became increasingly popular, particularly in Portugal and Spain. The use of a drug called laudanum, a liquid potion made from a mixture of opium and alcohol, was developed by Paracelsus (the common name of Swiss physician Bombast von Hohenheim). A German pharmacist named Wilhelm Serturner first isolated morphine from opium in 1803. He named it morphine after Morpheus, the Greek god of dreams.

IN THE SEVENTEENTH AND EIGHTEENTH CENTURIES PEOPLE OF ALL CLASSES BEGAN TO USE MORPHINE AS A RECREATIONAL DRUG.

the facts about HEROIN

By the end of the seventeenth century, the British had become heavily involved in the opium trade. The British imported opium from India and sold it to China. By the beginning of the second half of the eighteenth century, the British East India Company dominated the opium trade throughout the world. During the eighteenth and nineteenth centuries, they fought two wars with China over the powerful and lucrative crop. In fact, Hong Kong became part of the British Empire in 1841, when China lost the first Opium War.

"Heroic" Heroin

In the United States, opium abuse began to expand in the mid-1800s, largely through the opium dens opened by newly arrived Chinese immigrants who brought the drug into the country. During the American Civil War, the number of opium and morphine users and abusers grew as thousands of soldiers were treated with the drugs on the battlefield and took their addiction home with them. Many medicines were sold without prescription that contained laudanum and morphine, drawing thousands of others into the drugs' webs of dependence.

In 1874, British scientist C.R. Alder Wright combined opium with the chemical acetic anhydride in an attempt to find a non-addictive alternative to morphine. This created a white crystalline powder that, when injected, had the same pain-relieving, euphoria-inducing properties as opium and mor-

DURING THE CIVIL WAR, DOCTORS USED MORPHINE TO EASE SOLDIERS' PAIN. BUT WOUNDED SOLDIERS WERE NOT THE ONLY USERS OF THE DRUG. CASUAL USE OF DRUGS CONTAINING LAUDANUM AND MORPHINE WAS WIDESPREAD IN 19TH-CENTURY AMERICA.

phine. While working for the Bayer pharmaceutical laboratories of Germany, scientist Heinrich Dreser named this crystalline powder heroin, which he derived from the German word for heroic. Bayer laboratories—the same company that first manufactured and marketed aspirin—developed heroin as a medication for coughs, chest pains, and to relieve the pain of tuberculosis.

In 1890, the United States passed a law that imposed a tax on opium and morphine. Nevertheless,

the facts about HEROIN

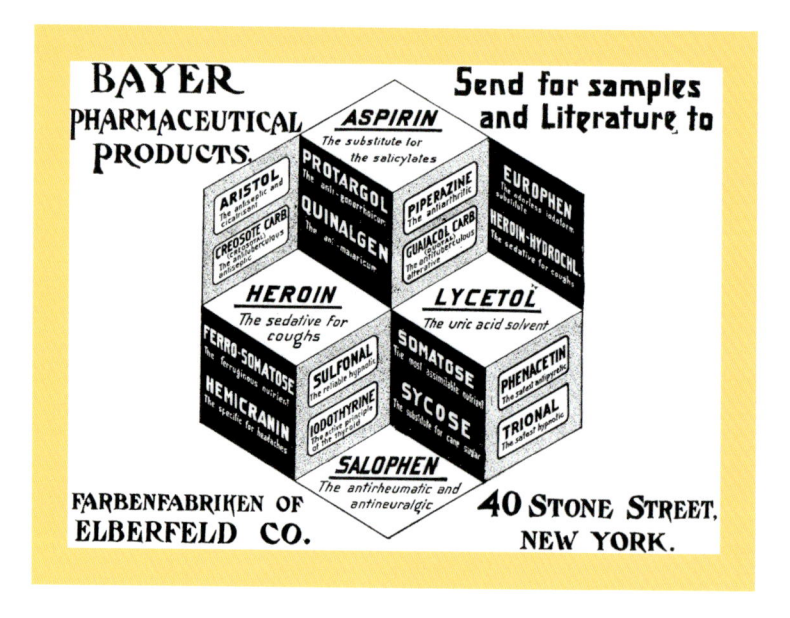

A 1900 BAYER PHARMACEUTICAL ADVERTISEMENT. BAYER INTRODUCED HEROIN IN 1898 AS A COUGH SUPPRESSANT.

Americans continued to consume opium, morphine, and heroin, even as more and more physicians were noting that their patients who took the drugs to relieve pain suffered severe symptoms when they stopped taking them. Finally, in 1905, the United States Congress banned opium. The following year, Congress passed the Pure Food and Drug Act, which required pharmaceutical companies to label their patent medicines with a list of all their ingredients. As a result of all these measures, the availability of opioid drugs dramatically declined. In 1914, Congress passed the Harrison Narcotics Tax Act, which required doctors, pharmacists, and others who prescribed narcotics to register and pay a tax.

These laws were just the first in a long line of legislation that attempted to slow the use of addictive substances. Despite these efforts, however, the use of heroin continues today, costing millions of dollars in law enforcement and health care, to say nothing of the personal tragedies experienced by individuals and their families caught up in the trap of heroin addiction.

Creating Heroin

The opium poppy, *Papaver somniferum*, is an annual plant, which means that it blooms just once, then dies. New seeds must be planted for the crop to grow again. The entire growth cycle is about 120 days. Just before reaching maturity, the poppy plant produces a flower. After about a week, the flower petals fall off, leaving a capsule. Raw opium gum is harvested from this capsule. The surface of the capsule is scored, or cut, with a knife containing three or four small blades, and the opium gum oozes out through these cuts. Each capsule is usually scored in this manner three to five times, or until scoring produces no more gum.

After the harvesting process is complete, the capsules are cut from the stem, allowed to dry, then broken open so that the seeds inside the capsule can be used for next year's crop. Once the gum is collected, the farmer sets it out to dry for several days, then wraps it in banana leaf or plastic. The farmer stores the gum until the trader comes to retrieve it. The trader then brings it to a refinery for processing.

Refining raw opium into heroin is a complicated process. Producers convert the opium into morphine by chemical processes that require several

To harvest opium, a sharp blade is used to extract the white, milky sap from mature poppy seed pods.

Jess, a seventeen-year-old high school junior, has taken heroin for a year. "I knew it was dangerous when I started, but I was hanging out with a group of older college students and they seemed to handle it okay." Like many new users, Jess thought if she didn't inject the drug, she wouldn't become an addict.

> *That first experience with heroin, I snorted it. It made me feel so good, so calm. I didn't feel nauseated at all, just warm. I used it once and then didn't use it again until the next weekend. And then the weekend after that, I had it both Friday and Saturday night. Pretty soon, I needed it almost every day, then every day. Within a month, I was hooked—even though I never injected.*

Jess still uses heroin every day. Her grades have plummeted, but her parents still don't know the root of the problem.

> *They just think I'm lazy when it comes to school, and they think I drink alcohol and maybe smoke pot. I hide my addiction really well. But I'm scared now. I get an allowance, a good one, but it's not enough to keep me in dope. I've started to steal money from my mom's purse to pay for my dope. I don't know how long I can keep this up without completely screwing up.*

the facts about HEROIN

Most illicit heroin varies in color from dark brown (left) to white (right). So-called black tar heroin (below), which comes from Mexico, is a sticky substance. Its color varies from dark brown to black.

basic elements and implements. Opium gum is dropped into 55-gallon drums of boiling water. The liquid is strained through burlap sacks, which leaves the morphine to dry. Once dried, the morphine is pressed into bricks.

Producers convert the morphine into heroin by mixing it with the chemicals acetic anhydride, sodium carbonate, activated charcoal, chloroform, ethyl alcohol, ether, and acetone. The two most commonly produced heroin varieties are No. 3 heroin, or smoking heroin, and No. 4 heroin, or injectable heroin.

Today, the heroin that emerges from most refineries is very pure—more than 90 percent pure by some estimates. As the heroin makes its way to the United States, however, it passes through many hands. Each person or organization in the distribution business adds substances to the product to make the heroin less pure and more bulky, adding to their profit as they sell the product by weight. These additives include caffeine, baking soda, powdered milk, and quinine. By the time the heroin gets to the user, it is often about 40 percent pure, and little is known about what makes up the other 60 percent of any given batch of heroin. The unknown purity and make-up of heroin add to the risk of taking the drug.

Using Heroin

There are four ways that people use heroin: they inject it using hypodermic needles after mixing the heroin with water, they snort the powder itself, they smoke it by inhaling smoke from heated powder, or they swallow it. Injecting the drug directly into a vein (intravenous injection) provides the greatest intensity and most rapid onset of effects. Intravenously-injected heroin takes affect within about eight seconds. Injecting the drug into muscles (intramuscular injection) causes the effects to occur within five to eight minutes. When a person smokes or sniffs the drug, he or she starts to feel the effects after about ten to fifteen minutes.

Soon after a user takes heroin in any manner, the drug crosses the blood-brain barrier. Once inside the brain, heroin then attaches to certain brain cells called opioid receptors. Almost immediately, in just about eight seconds after intravenous injection, the user feels a rush of pleasurable sensations, along with warm flushing of the skin, dry mouth, and a heavy feeling in the body. Most first-time users also feel nausea and experience vomiting, though these effects usually do not recur with continued use.

Because heroin acts as a depressive on the nervous system, the user's heart rate slows, blood pressure lowers, breathing becomes slower and shallower, and mental functioning decreases. This so-called slow-down makes one feel completely relaxed, which is in part what makes heroin use so desirable to many users.

However, this same slowdown can be fatal if a user takes too much of the drug or if the drug he or she injects is particularly potent. In such cases, the heart can stop beating altogether, causing death. In addition to the effects of the drug itself, heroin may have additives that do not readily dissolve, resulting in clogged blood vessels that lead to the lungs, liver, kidney, or brain. This can result in infection or death of tissue. Furthermore, heroin users may have used other types of drugs at the same time, including alcohol, cocaine, and other opioids. Combining heroin with other substances is particularly popular among users, and particularly dangerous.

A heroin user may use the drug up to four times a day. Dependence on and tolerance of the drug usually develops. Tolerance means that the user requires more of the drug to feel its effects at the same level. Dependence occurs when the body adapts to the

INJECTION IS THE MOST COMMON METHOD OF ADMINISTERING HEROIN. CONTINUED USE IN THIS MANNER CAN LEAD TO COLLAPSED VEINS AND INCREASES THE USER'S RISK OF CONTRACTING POTENTIALLY DEADLY DISEASES LIKE AIDS AND HEPATITIS C.

presence of the drug so that the user will experience discomfort and even illness whenever the level of the drug in his or her body falls below a certain level. Called withdrawal, this side effect of heroin abuse is one reason that heroin is such an addictive drug: it is simply too painful, physically and psychologically, to stop using the drug. Major withdrawal symptoms peak between forty-eight and seventy-two hours after the last dose of heroin and subside after about a week.

After months or years of chronic heroin use, a user may suffer from a variety of physical, psychological, and social effects. The complications of heroin use and abuse can and often do destroy an abuser's life—or end it entirely. A heroin user who injects the drug also risks contracting such potentially deadly diseases as AIDS, hepatitis B and C, and liver disease.

The Blood-Brain Barrier

Opiates like heroin affect the brain because they are able to cross what's called the "blood-brain barrier," a physiological obstacle between blood vessels in the central nervous system and the central nervous system itself. This barrier stops many substances from traveling across it, thus protecting the brain from many harmful substances. However, opiates do pass through the barrier and thus are able to interact with cells to trigger their effects on the brain and body.

SHORT-TERM EFFECTS	LONG-TERM EFFECTS
Rush	Addiction
Pain Relief	Infectious diseases such as HIV/AIDS, and hepatitis B and C
Euphoria	
Depressed respiration	Collapsed veins
Clouded mental functioning	Bacterial infections
Nausea and vomiting	Abscesses
Spontaneous abortion in pregnant women	Infection of the heart lining and valves
	Liver disease
	Arthritis and other rheumatic problems

Heroin use, as is the case with all illicit drug use, is a problem for the criminal justice system as well. The U.S. Drug Enforcement Administration (DEA) made 2,329 heroin-related arrests in 2003 on the federal level. Heroin-related arrests on the state level numbered in the hundreds of thousands. According to statistics from the Arrestee Drug Abuse Monitoring Program, about 5.8 percent of men and 6.6 percent of women arrested during

the facts about HEROIN

2003 tested positive for opiates at arrest. This statistic indicates the level to which heroin abuse can lead to other crimes, either in order to pay to maintain the habit or because of the recklessness that often accompanies illicit drug use.

Heroin Use Today

Heroin use continues to decline in the United States. According to the Monitoring the Future study conducted by the University of Michigan in 2003, rates of heroin use among teens are almost 50 percent lower than peak rates in prior decades. Among eighth, tenth, and twelfth graders, only about 1.5 percent have ever used heroin. Moreover, 63 percent of eighth graders, 71 percent of tenth graders, and 59 percent of twelfth graders said that they thought that using

2003 HEROIN USE BY STUDENTS

STUDENTS	EVER USED	USED IN THE PAST YEAR	USED IN THE PAST MONTH
8TH GRADERS	1.6%	0.9%	0.4%
10TH GRADERS	1.5%	0.7%	0.3%
12TH GRADERS	1.5%	0.8%	0.4%

Source: Monitoring the Future study

heroin just once—even without injecting it—was a "great risk."

Nevertheless, heroin remains readily available to young people. The Monitoring the Future study showed that 15.6 percent of eighth graders, 18.8 percent of tenth graders, and 27.9 percent of twelfth graders surveyed reported that heroin was "fairly easy" or "very easy" to obtain. The use of heroin remains a medical, social, and legal problem in this country, including among the teenage population.

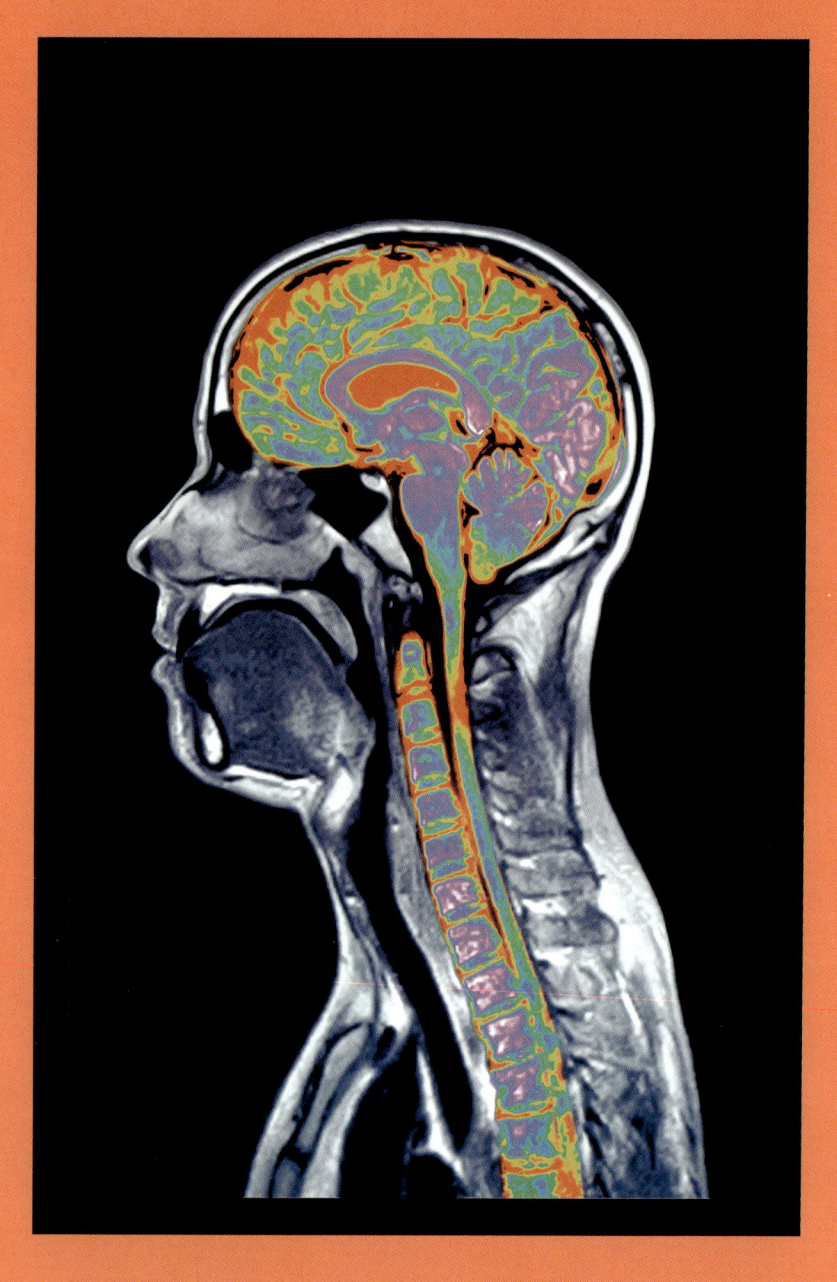

THE CENTRAL NERVOUS SYSTEM IS MADE UP OF THE BRAIN AND SPINAL CORD, SHOWN HERE IN AN MRI SCAN. HEROIN AND OTHER OPIATES STIMULATE THE BRAIN'S "PLEASURE SYSTEM."

2 What Heroin Does

ALL OF THE WAYS in which heroin and other opiates affect the brain are not known, but it is now clear that opiates stimulate what scientists call "the pleasure system" in the brain. This system involves several different types of neurotransmitters, or brain chemicals, including dopamine and endorphins.

The human brain and nervous system form a vast communications network. Every emotion we feel, action we take, and physiological function we undergo is processed through the brain and the nerve fibers that extend down the spinal cord and through the body.

The brain itself is divided into several large regions, each responsible for performing certain activities. The cerebral cortex is the largest and most highly developed portion of the brain. Divided into four lobes, the cortex is the center of the brain's higher powers, where "thinking" activity—thought, perception, memory, and communication—takes place. Other parts of the brain control more basic physiological functions, such as breathing, blood pressure, and digestion, by sending signals to the lungs, the heart and blood vessels, and the stomach, to name just a few.

For all of this to occur, brain cells must be able to communicate with one another to send messages from one cell to another, from one center of brain activity to the next. Heroin and other opiates interfere with, and may even permanently alter, this communications network.

Getting the Message Across: The Synapse

To understand how information is received in the human brain and processed to trigger emotions like excitement and joy, scientists study not only the anatomy of the brain—its large structures and organization—but also the biochemical processes that take place among the tiniest cells of the nervous system, called neurons.

Each neuron contains three important parts: the cell body, the dendrites, and the axon. Messages from other neurons enter the cell body through the dendrites, which are branch-like projections that extend from the cell body. Once the cell body processes the messages, it can pass on the information

What Heroin Does

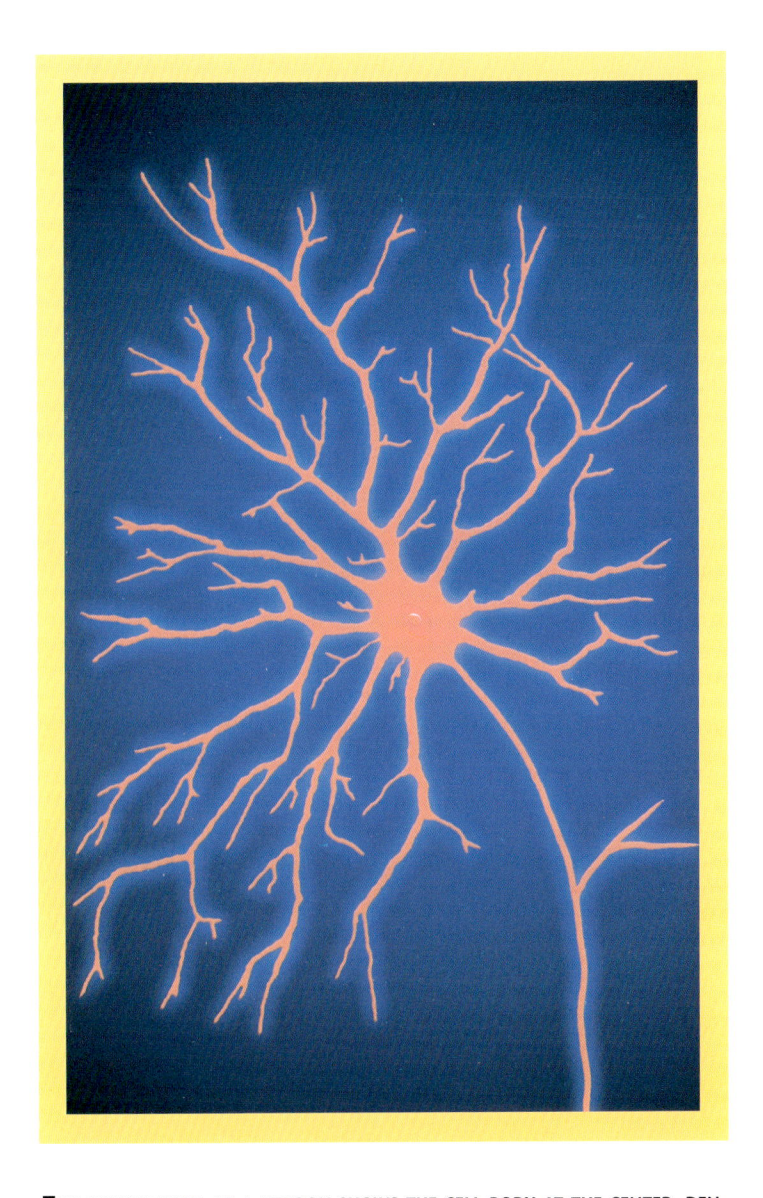

This illustration of a neuron shows the cell body at the center, dendrites branching out from the cell body, and a single long axon extending from the cell (lower right).

to its neighboring neuron through a cable-like fiber called the axon. At speeds faster than one can imagine, information about every aspect of human physiology, emotion, and thought zips through the body from one neuron to another in this manner.

But the axon of one neuron does not attach directly to its neighboring neuron. Instead, a tiny gap—called a synapse—separates them. For a message to cross a synapse, it requires the help of natural chemicals called neurotransmitters, which are stored in packets at the end of each nerve cell.

When a cell is ready to send a message, its axon releases a certain amount and type of neurotransmitter. This chemical then travels across the synapse to bind to special molecules, called receptors, which sit

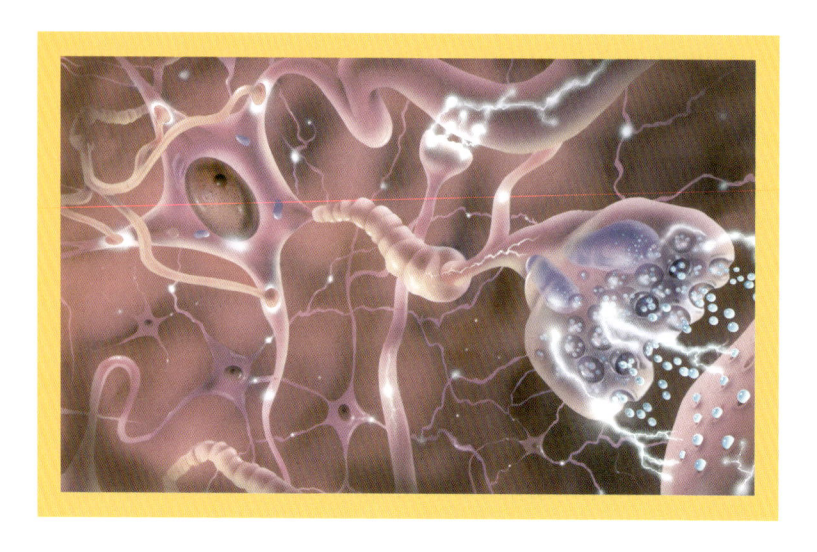

AN ILLUSTRATION OF A NEURON SENDING A NERVE IMPULSE. ONE CELL'S AXONS RELEASE NEUROTRANSMITTERS ACROSS THE SYNAPSE TO ANOTHER CELL'S DENDRITES.

on the surfaces of all cells in the body and bind to specific chemicals. Receptors are very complex structures. They have sites into which a very specific neurotransmitter molecule can fit. This works in a similar fashion to a lock-and-key mechanism. The neurotransmitter molecules from the first molecule are the keys and the receptors on the second molecule are the locks. When the key enters the lock by binding to the receptor molecule, the transmission of the message is complete. In this way, the brain sends signals to all parts of the body through its vast system of nerve cells.

The neurotransmitters most affected by heroin and other opiates include endorphins, enkephalins, and dynorphin, often collectively known as endogenous, or internally-occurring, opioids. Endogenous opioids work to regulate vital functions such as hunger and thirst, and are involved in mood control, immune system responses, and other processes.

The reason that opiates such as heroin and morphine affect us so powerfully is that these substances bind to the same receptors as the endogenous opioids, and therefore have widespread effects on the body. Of particular importance is heroin's similarity to the opioids called endorphins, which the brain manufactures to provide relief when the body experiences pain or stress. Endorphins flood the space between nerve cells and inhibit the firing of nerve impulse, which creates an analgesic, or pain-killing effect. The brain floods with endorphins when the body exercises, for instance, resulting in the "runner's high" many athletes experience.

Similarly, the heroin molecule locks onto the endorphin receptor sites on nerve endings in the pleasure part of the brain, leading to intense feelings of euphoria and well-being. Involved in this response is another neurotransmitter called dopamine. Dopamine is a key element in the body's response to pleasure. An increased amount of opioids in the brain increases the amount of dopamine, which in turn heightens the sense of well-being and reward experienced by the user.

In addition to the pleasure/pain centers, there is also a concentration of opiate receptors in the area of the brain that helps to control respiration. When opiates attach to cells here, they act to slow down breathing as well as to inhibit the impulse to cough. These effects help explain why opium and morphine were popular remedies for tuberculosis, and why another opiate—codeine—continues to be an ingredient in prescription cough remedies today. However, if this center is exposed to very high levels of opiates, respiration can cease altogether, leading to death. A third location for opiate receptors is in the brain's vomiting center. Opiate use often induces nausea and vomiting, though users tend to build up a tolerance for this effect very quickly.

Other Opiates

Many people looking for that "heroin high" without a supply of the drug often look to other substances that have similar effects. Called opiate analogs, these drugs have chemical structures similar to that of morphine and heroin. Three of the most common opiate analogs are the following:

Fentanyl. Known on the street as "China White," fentanyl is perhaps the most common of the synthetic opiates. Introduced in 1968 by a Belgian pharmaceutical company, fentanyl is prescribed as a painkiller for patients undergoing surgery. Fentanyl and its analogs are about eighty times stronger than morphine. According to the National Institute on Drug Abuse, about 150 people die every year from fentanyl overdoses. Fentanyl kills by slowing down a user's breathing until it stops completely. The drug may also cause the chest muscles to contract so tightly that the lungs cannot expand to take in air. Those who overdose from it simply suffocate to death.

Oxycodone. A very strong pain medication, oxycodone is a synthetic form of morphine that comes in tablet form. Some users swallow the pills whole, while others crush them, then snort the powder or inject the powder after mixing it with water. Oxycodone is sold by prescription under the name Percodan.

Meperidine. More commonly known as Demerol, meperidine is another very strong pain reliever similar in structure to morphine. It is often prescribed to patients immediately following surgery or for terminally ill cancer patients suffering chronic pain related to their disease. Directly related to meperiidine is another analog, called MPTP, also known as the "new heroin." Side effects of MPTP may be quite severe and often permanent. They involve symptoms of Parkinson's disease, which include nerve and muscle damage that cause slowness of movement, tremors, and rigidity.

Taking Heroin

Heroin usually comes as a powder. In its purest form, it is white, but depending on the various substances manufacturers produce it with the color of the powder may be pink, gray, or brown. More rarely, heroin comes in tablet form. Users take heroin in four different ways:

Injecting. After dissolving the powder in water mixed with citric acid and heating, users draw the liquid into a syringe and inject it. Some users "skin pop," which involves injecting the drug right under the skin, while others inject into the muscles or directly into a vein.

Snorting or sniffing. Sniffing the powder into the nose puts heroin in direct contact with the blood vessels that line the nose so that the drug enters the bloodstream fairly quickly. Users who snort or sniff heroin feel its effects within about ten to fifteen minutes. This method of taking heroin has increased in popularity because it does not require using needles and thus does not put the user at risk for HIV or hepatitis infection.

Smoking. With this method, also called "chasing the dragon," users smoke heroin by first placing the powder on metal foil and then heating it from underneath with a match or a lighter. Smoke is released that users inhale through a straw. Once in the lungs, the heroin is quickly absorbed into the thin lining of the blood vessels.

Swallowing. This method is extremely dangerous, because no one knows how much a person can ingest without overdosing. And because most of the drug is destroyed in the stomach before it can enter the bloodstream and reach the brain, swallowing the drug is the least common way to take heroin.

Heroin is the fastest-acting of all opiates. When intravenously injected, it reaches the brain within seven to eight seconds. Smoked heroin reaches the brain in about ten to fifteen minutes, but the peak experience of smoking lasts only a few minutes. Injecting the drug leads to about an hour of intense pleasure, starting with a rush of warmth and euphoria followed by a period of peacefulness and often drowsiness (called being "on the nod") that lasts about an hour. For perhaps another hour or so, feelings of well-being and control persist. During this period, some users want to be by themselves, in their own world. Others find themselves feeling more sociable and stimulated. The effects of the drug usually wear off within five hours, depending on the dose.

Injecting heroin offers users the quickest and most intense "high." However, in recent years, snorting or smoking heroin has become more popular. Many users, particularly young people, mistakenly believe that as long as a user doesn't inject the drug, he or she cannot become addicted. In fact, not only is heroin an addictive substance no matter how it is ingested, studies show that most regular users who snort or smoke the drug soon start to inject the drug. Another reason for the increased popularity of snorting or smoking, rather than injecting, heroin is that the quality of the heroin—the strength of the product sold on the street—has increased dramatically over the years.

The Heroin Experience
The first time someone uses heroin, the effects can be quite unpleasant. Because the drug affects the vomiting center in the brain, most first time users experience nausea and vomiting. Once the nausea passes, the drug's more pleasurable effects take hold. These effects begin with a "rush," which lasts from one to two minutes following the drug's entry into the brain. This rush is more intense when the user injects the heroin, but those who snort it also describe having this feeling. After the rush comes a "high," described by users as a pervasive warm and pleasurable feeling that lasts for four to five hours. The high is caused by the heroin diffusing from the bloodstream into the brain.

Over time, addicts often find that heroin fails to trigger either the rush or the high, so they continue to take the drug only to stave off withdrawal symptoms. A heroin abuser typically injects up to four times a day in order to keep himself or herself from the feelings of nausea, muscle pain, weakness, and irritation associated with withdrawal.

Mixing Drugs

No hard and fast statistics exist, but experts in the field of drug abuse agree that most people who use heroin often combine heroin with other substances, particularly cocaine, tranquilizers, amphetamines, and alcohol. They do so for several reasons: sometimes to heighten the effects of heroin, sometimes to maintain a high when no heroin is available, sometimes to help them cope with withdrawal. Mixing heroin with other drugs heightens both the "high" and the risk from the heroin itself. Pairing heroin with other central nervous system depressants, such as alcohol and barbiturates, is a very common cause of overdose. Respiration and heart rate drops quickly and dramatically, causing breathing to cease, the heart to stop, and—without immediate medical intervention—death. Another popular but potentially deadly combination is cocaine and heroin. Here are some of the most common combinations:

Alcohol. Both alcohol and heroin depress the central nervous system, and the combination may prove fatal.

Amphetamines. Amphetamines are stimulants, and their stimulant effects may mask the opiate effects of heroin, making heroin overdoses more likely.

"The first time I used heroin, about two years ago, I didn't know what I was taking," Keisha, now a twenty-one-year-old high school senior, admits.

> I thought it was cocaine, which I'd been snorting since I was about fourteen. I was in such a bad place then, and I really didn't care what happened to me. I'd run away from home and was living on the street. I was prostituting myself for drugs. I wasn't picky about what I put in my body, to say the least. I wasn't paying attention and someone gave me brown powder instead of white powder. It was the worst thing that could have happened to me.
>
> I didn't throw up—I guess that happens more often when you inject it—but I felt nauseated. But then I felt so mellow, so at ease. It seemed like I felt relaxed for the first time since I entered adolescence. And that made me want to feel that feeling again, all the time. I still partied with other drugs, but heroin became my best friend. I could do it when I was alone, too, which I did more and more often as the addiction set in.

Keisha's mother tried to get her help, but Keisha ran away from the two substance abuse programs she entered. "That's when I started living on the streets. I couldn't go home and I didn't want help. And I needed money to eat—though I didn't eat much—and to support my habit." It wasn't until Keisha was arrested that she "snapped to it."

> I come from a middle class family. I was in accelerated classes in school. I woke up to how uncool—and dangerous—prostituting myself and injecting heroin really was. I went into a ninety-day, in-house program and stayed there. My addiction isn't over. It never will be. But I've been clean for three years now and, today, I intend to stay that way.

Cocaine. A mixture of heroin and cocaine—known as a "speedball"—is especially dangerous. The two drugs together act to enhance the effect of each one: the cocaine acts as a powerful stimulant, which raises the heartbeat. But its effects wear off quicker than heroin, which in turn slows the heart. As a result, the heart can lose its rhythm entirely. Both John Belushi and River Phoenix died after taking speedballs.

Ecstasy. This "club drug," known by its chemical acronym MDMA, is both a depressant and mild hallucinogen. Taking heroin with Ecstasy may mask opiate effects of heroin, triggering a user to take more of the drug and risk overdose.

GHB (Gamma hydroxy butyrate). Another synthetic drug, GHB is a liquid sedative anesthetic. Mixing it with heroin could fatally depress the central nervous system.

LSD. Hallucinogenic drugs disrupt brain chemistry in a variety of ways. Using LSD with heroin can make heroin's effects both unpredictable and unpleasant.

Whether taken alone or in combination with other drugs, heroin is highly addictive and harmful to the user. Addiction to any illegal substance carries with it enormous psychological, legal, and social consequences. The health risks of heroin addiction, especially when users inject the drug, are extremely complex and challenging.

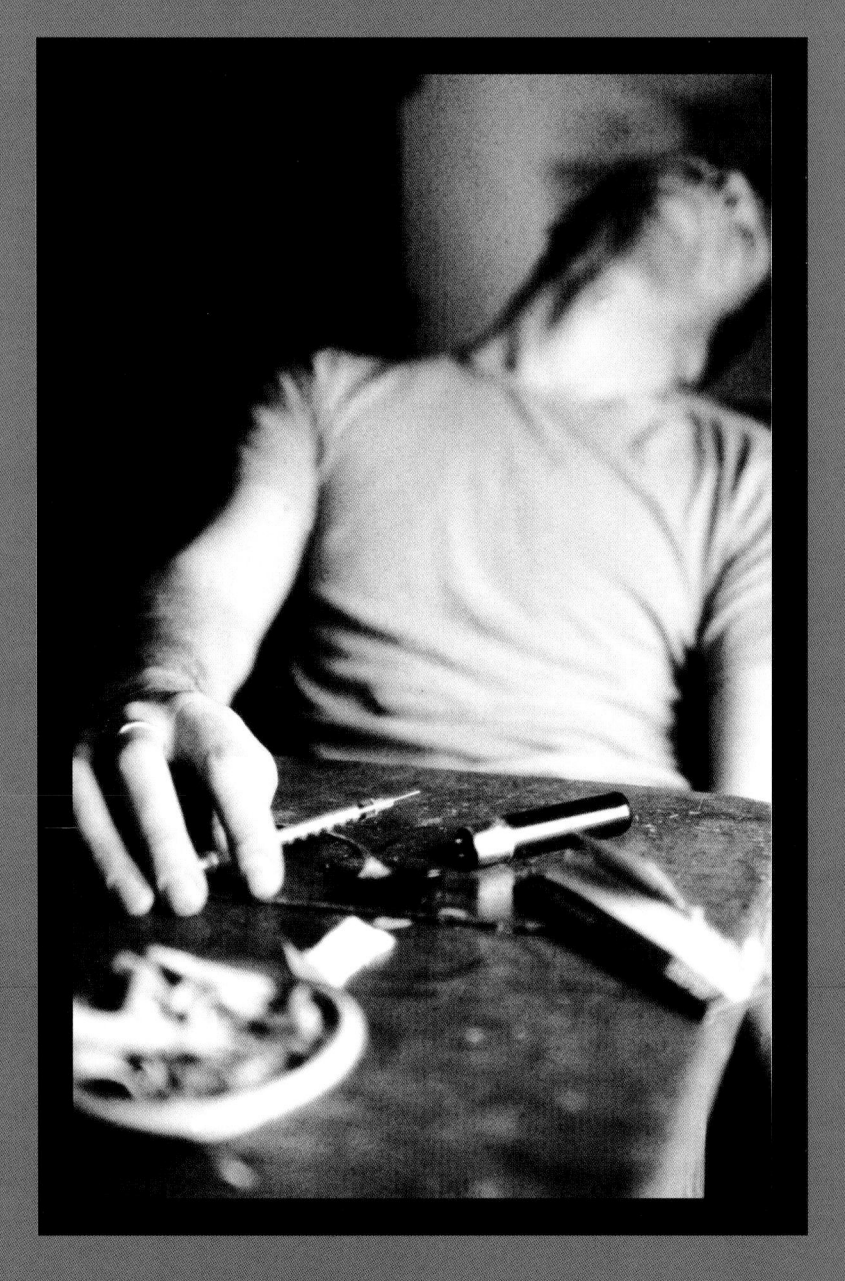

After injecting, a heroin user experiences a surge of euphoria. Then all of the body's processes slow down. A period of drowsiness ensues, which is commonly called being on the nod.

3 The Dangers of Use and Abuse

THAT FIRST RUSH, it was the warmest, most *peaceful feeling I'd ever had. Floating away from everything. Better than anything. I can't even describe the peace I felt.* This is how heroin users have described the emotional and physical effects of this drug, especially when they first start using it. Hearing about these reactions, along with the desire to engage in risky behaviors so common among teens, prompts many teens to try heroin for the first time.

Most people who decide to experiment with heroin are soon describing their experience in very different terms. "Craving the drug, needing it, until nothing mattered anymore." "Life without energy, life without interests—other than the drug. I only had a half life, if that." "I watched my skin break out. I couldn't eat, and I got so thin. My eyes were bloodshot all the time. I looked old and tired and I was only twenty years old."

The Medical Consequences of Heroin Abuse

The effects of heroin on the body are widespread. Some effects are merely uncomfortable and unsightly; others are quite severe and can be deadly. First, the drug itself slows down all body processes, from respiration and heart rate to digestion and immune system response. The results of this effect are numerous and include a higher risk of pneumonia and other lung infections, constipation, dramatic weight loss due to loss of appetite, and chronic physical exhaustion.

Heroin abuse also results in mental health issues. The drug itself disrupts the chemistry within the brain's mood centers, leading to depression and mood swings. Additionally, possessing heroin is illegal so those who use and abuse the drug often lead double lives. They hide their criminal activity from their families, teachers, and employers. Such stress weighs heavily on a user's self-esteem.

Women who use heroin put themselves at special risk: prolonged use can disrupt their menstrual cycles and, if they are pregnant, using heroin puts their unborn children at grave risk of miscarriage, low birthweight, and addiction to heroin at birth.

Other adverse effects occur because the heroin that users buy on the street is rarely pure. Sellers often mix it with impurities such as talcum powder, baking soda, and other substances, which, when injected into the body, cause serious side effects. Skin infections and abscesses are common. If the user injects the drug, blistering and scabbing around the injection sites often result. Infections of the lining of the heart and blood vessels may occur, along with liver disease, which causes the jaundice (yellowness of the skin) seen in so many heroin abusers. The additives themselves may clog the blood vessels that lead to the lungs, liver, kidneys, and brain. The fact that users who buy heroin on the street have no way to judge the purity of the product they buy causes another problem: If the heroin is particularly strong, users can inject too much of the drug and overdose.

Heroin users who inject the drug often share needles and syringes. Such activity leads to the spread of a host of infections, including the potentially fatal diseases HIV and hepatitis.

Heroin and HIV and AIDS

The human immunodeficiency virus (HIV) was first isolated in the early 1980s after several young men and women died of unusual illnesses, illnesses that their natural disease-fighting systems normally would have been able to fight. Scientists discovered that a virus was attacking certain cells of the

the facts about HEROIN

SOME DRUG ADDICTS COLLECT DISCARDED NEEDLES AND USE THEM TO INJECT THEM-SELVES. THIS PRACTICE OF SHARING NEEDLES LEADS TO THE SPREAD OF DISEASE.

immune system, the part of the body that attacks the harmful materials that can harm healthy cells. When the virus has destroyed enough of these vital immune system cells, an infected person develops acquired immunodeficiency syndrome (AIDS). Although medication is now available to slow down or even prevent the HIV virus from destroying the immune system, AIDS remains a serious, life-threatening condition.

According to the Centers for Disease Control and Prevention, up to 36 percent of all new infections with HIV occur among injecting drug users, which puts heroin abusers at special risk. There are two ways that heroin use can lead to HIV infection.

Using or sharing contaminated needles, cotton swabs, rinse water, and cookers when injecting heroin or other drugs leaves a drug user vulnerable to contracting or transmitting HIV.

And the sexual behavior of heroin users also contributes to the spread of HIV. In a study published in 2002 issue of *Drug and Alcohol Dependence*, sexually active drug users, including those who used heroin by itself and those who used both heroin and cocaine, engaged in a variety of sex risks associated with HIV infection. Those behaviors included having sex with multiple partners, sex with an injectable-drug user, and exchanging sex for drugs or money. More than 80 percent of drug users who were sexually active reported having sex without using a condom in the previous twenty days.

Hepatitis C

Hepatitis C virus (HCV) is the most common chronic blood-borne infection in the United States. Unlike other types of hepatitis, there is no vaccine to prevent hepatitis C infection. According to the National Institutes of Health, approximately four million Americans have been infected with the virus. The virus is particularly prevalent among injection drug users who practice such risky behaviors as sharing syringes and other paraphernalia. In fact, during the past decade, injection drug use has become the major mode of hepatitis C transmission in the United States, accounting for at least 60 percent of transmitted cases.

Currently, there is no standard effective treatment for HCV infection. A combination of antiviral drugs has helped some of those infected, but improvement is seen only while patients take the drugs. Although some people infected with HCV are able to fight it off naturally, most (about 75 to

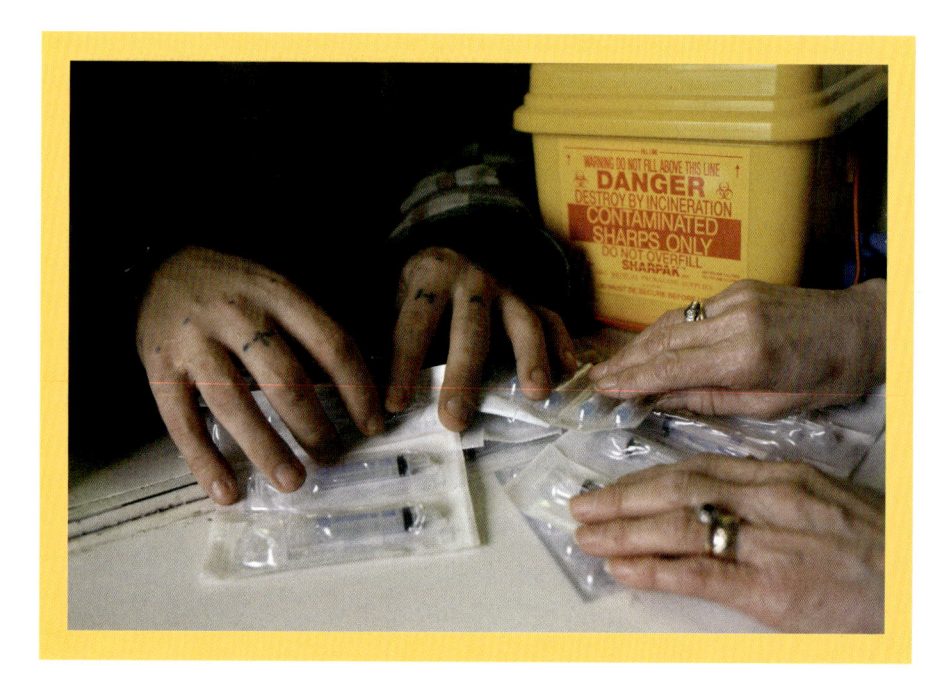

A CLINIC WORKER DISTRIBUTES STERILE SYRINGES TO AN INTRAVENOUS DRUG USER. NEARLY 30 PERCENT OF NEW AIDS CASES IN THE UNITED STATES CAN BE TRACED TO THE SHARING OF SYRINGES BY INJECTION DRUG USERS.

85 percent, according to the National Institutes of Health) develop chronic infection. Although most suffer no symptoms, complications can occur at any time—even decades after initial infection. As liver cells die, a life-threatening condition known as cirrhosis occurs, in which scar tissue develops in the liver, preventing normal blood flow. About 10 to 20 percent of people infected with HCV develop cirrhosis and another one to five percent of those infected develop primary liver cancer.

Heroin and Mood Disorders

Heroin acts as a depressant on the body, slowing down the way most body processes work. Blood pressure and heart rate decrease, as does respiration, which can lead to sudden death if addicts use too much heroin, or use it in combination with other drugs, or if the strength of the heroin is stronger than they are used to.

But that's not the only way that heroin acts as a depressant: it also depresses mood, and continued use may lead to clinical depression due to changes in the brain caused by heroin. Depression and anxiety in heroin users sometimes develops because of the shame that they feel about the illegal nature of their habit, the lies they must tell friends and family in order to continue their lifestyle, and the difficulties they have in maintaining certain aspects of their life, such as going to school, keeping a job, and enjoying hobbies.

"I screwed up my life as a teenager, there's no doubt about that, but I thought when I got straight, I'd be fine. I was wrong." admits Troy, now a twenty-four-year-old college sophomore who has just been diagnosed with Hepatitis C.

Troy was ten years old when his history with drug addiction began. His 17-year-old cousin shared a joint of marijuana with him and the experience changed him forever.

I'm not one of those guys who thinks marijuana leads to worse drugs—I don't know about that. All I know is that that first hit of dope let me forget what was going on around me and the more I smoked, the less I had to deal with it. And everyone else was doing it, so why not? But it wasn't enough for me, I guess. I wanted to try more stuff; I wanted to live dangerously. So then I started fooling with coke. And that was crazy. I really got hooked on that stuff.

Like many people who use cocaine, which is a powerful stimulant, Troy turned to heroin to bring him down from that high, to "even out," as he put it.

"I was the oh-so-typical 'rebel without a cause,' dropping out of school at fifteen, running away from home, living on the streets, committing crimes. It was a nightmare. I was a nightmare." Troy grew up in a rough part of a small southern city and never thought he had a future. "My father left when I was born. I never knew him. My mom used drugs when I was little, but she got herself clean when I went to school. All I saw around me was drugs and poverty and hopelessness. I didn't think there was any other way to live."

Troy's whole world revolved around drugs. All of his friends were involved in the scene, too, and many of those associates injected heroin. "I kept snorting heroin— more and more of it—trying to get the feeling the first few hits of heroin gave me. Didn't work. So a buddy lent me some works (needles, syringes, and spoons) and the next time I had some heroin, I injected it."

Troy was 19 when he was arrested for possession of heroin. He faced four years in jail if convicted. Luckily, the court offered him an intensive probation through a "drug court." He could stay out of jail, but he would have to report to a probation officer and take a drug test every week. He also had to join a twelve-step rehabilitation program such as Alcoholics Anonymous or NarcAnon.

That's the option I took. I got a doctor, who helped me through the withdrawal and then I worked the program. I've been clean five years and now I'm in college. I want to be a social worker, to work with kids like me, to show them that there's hope and help them find the tools they need.

But Troy has another consequence of his drug use to face: a diagnosis of hepatitis C, a debilitating and potentially fatal disease affecting the liver.

When I first heard the news, I was almost glad because I was most afraid I'd gotten HIV. But HCV isn't a picnic either. I've got to see a doctor regularly, take medication, and try to stay as healthy as I can. And hope it doesn't get worse. Luckily, I'd already given up the drugs and the alcohol, which really hurt your liver, so now I'm just going to live as best I can and look to the future.

Although most heroin overdoses occur by accident, according to a study by scientists at the University of New South Wales, Australia, heroin users have a 14 percent higher rate of suicide than those who do not use drugs. Lowering the risk of depression and suicide in heroin users, as well as recovering addicts, remains a challenge to users and those who treat them.

Withdrawal: The Body Rebels
When users stop taking heroin, morphine, or another opiate after using it for weeks or months, they usually experience painful and intense symptoms. Called withdrawal, these effects are the body's reaction to the loss of this powerful actor in its chemistry and physiology. Withdrawal, which in regular abusers may occur as early as a few hours after the last administration, produces drug craving, restlessness, muscle and bone pain, insomnia, diarrhea and vomiting, cold flashes with goose bumps, kicking movements, and other symptoms.

All of these symptoms are related to the body's reaction to the loss of this powerful depressant, whose presence has muted the body's ordinary responses. For instance, one common withdrawal symptom is anxiety. Researchers believe that people withdrawing from heroin experience anxiety partly because a section of the brain affected by heroin—called the locus coeruleus—becomes hyperactive during withdrawal. When heroin is present in the brain, it depresses the activity of the locus coeruleus, which is an important center of the brain's "fear-alarm system." When the depressive effects of heroin disappear, this part of the brain becomes activated again, resulting in marked anxiety and agitation.

SYMPTOMS OF HEROIN WITHDRAWAL

- Dilated pupils
- Goose bumps
- Watery eyes
- Runny nose
- Tremors
- Panic
- Chills
- Nausea
- Muscle cramps
- Insomnia
- Anxiety

Most withdrawal symptoms peak between forty-eight and seventy-two hours after the last dose and subside after about a week. A user can greatly lessen withdrawal symptoms if he or she slowly tapers doses of heroin over days or weeks, or by working with a physician to switch to methadone, a medication with properties similar to heroin but without its serious side effects. Physicians may also prescribe anti-anxiety medications, such as diazepam (Valium) to ease the extreme anxiety associated with opiate withdrawal.

Rarely, and only among heavily addicted people in already ill health, is withdrawal fatal. The psychological hold that heroin has on those who use and abuse it, however, is the most difficult effect to overcome.

Overdose: A Fatal Side Effect
Fatal overdoses of heroin occur when the amount of heroin taken causes extreme reactions in the body. An overdose of heroin will cause rapid heart beat, heart failure, shortness of breath, ringing in the ears or head, convulsions, unconsciousness, and coma. If untreated, overdoses may cause death. Overdoses of heroin also commonly occur when a user mixes heroin with other substances, such as alcohol, cocaine, or depressants such as Valium or oxycodone.

Addiction

Scientists still do not fully understand the mechanism of addiction, or the physiological and psychological need to use a drug that develops over time. Many believe that there are two basic components to drug addiction: tolerance and dependence.

Tolerance is the user's need to use more of the drug in order to experience the same effects. This need grows gradually as the body adapts to the presence of the drug in the brain and attempts to correct the chemical imbalance it creates. Dependence occurs when the brain's own chemistry becomes altered after it has received a steady supply of heroin. When a user stops taking the drug, the once-inhibited neurons start pumping out neurotransmitters again, causing a chemical imbalance in the brain. This imbalance leads to heroin withdrawal symptoms. *Merriam-Webster's Dictionary*] defines addiction as:

> a compulsive need for and use of a habit-forming substance (as heroin, nicotine, or alcohol) characterized by tolerance and by well-defined physiological symptoms upon withdrawal; persistent compulsive use of a substance known by the user to be harmful.

Another definition of addiction comes from the *Diagnostic and Statistical Manual of Mental Disorders*

Famous Lives Destroyed by Heroin Use

1958 Billie Holiday
Ms. Holiday died from complications due to a combination of heroin and alcohol addiction while under arrest in a hospital bed in New York City.

1970 Janis Joplin
Ms. Joplin was just twenty-seven years old when she died of a heroin overdose in Los Angeles.

1970 Jimi Hendrix
This rock legend died of a barbiturate overdose, but he'd long been a known heroin user. He was twenty-seven years old.

1977 Sid Vicious
A few months after stabbing his girlfriend Nancy Spungen to death in New York's Chelsea Hotel, punk rocker Sid Vicious died of a heroin overdose at the age of twenty-one.

1982 James Honeyman-Scott
1983 Pete Farndon
Two members of rock group The Pretenders died as a result of speedball overdoses within a year of each other.

1991 Johnny Thunders
In New Orleans in 1991, guitarist Johnny Thunders of New York Dolls and the Heartbreakers fame, died of a heroin overdose.

1994 Kurt Cobain
The Seattle-based Nirvana guitarist-vocalist Cobain shot himself after years of heroin abuse.

1994 Kristin Pfaff
Twenty-seven-year-old bassist in Courtney Love's band, Hole, died of a heroin overdose.

1995 Jonathan Melvoin
Guitarist for Smashing Pumpkins died of a heroin overdose.

KURT COBAIN

(fourth edition), a reference tool used by psychiatrists and other health professionals in diagnosing and treating mental illness. This manual defines addiction as a pattern of behavior, occurring over a period of twelve or more months, that includes at least three of the following:

- substance is often taken in larger amounts or over longer periods of time than intended;
- persistent desire or unsuccessful efforts to cut down or control substance use;
- a great deal of time is spent in activities necessary to obtain the substance (e.g., visiting multiple doctors or driving long distances), use the substance (e.g., chain smoking), or recover from its effects;
- important social, occupational, or recreational activities given up or reduced because of substance abuse;
- continued substance use despite knowledge of having a persistent or recurrent psychological, or physical problem that is caused or exacerbated by use of the substance.

In addition to exhibiting these behaviors, an addicted person will also develop tolerance to the drug, which the manual defines as either the need for ready amounts of the substance in order to achieve intoxication or desired effects, or markedly diminished effect with continued use of the same amount of the substance. Finally, symptoms of withdrawal from the drug must be present, which is defined as being either characteristic withdrawal syndrome for the substance or use of the same (or closely related) substance to relieve or avoid withdrawal symptoms.

In addition to these devastating physical affects, heroin users often suffer other consequences. The manufacture, sale, and use of heroin are all illegal in the United States.

Afghanistan is one of the world's leading producers of heroin and other drugs. Here, an Afghan man pours gasoline onto a pile of seized drugs, including 375 pounds (170 kilograms) of heroin.

4 The Traffic and the Law

FOR CENTURIES, the heroin trade was a highly lucrative one, so lucrative that it caused two wars between Great Britain and China in the nineteenth century. Although the trade is illegal today, it continues to rage throughout the world, from southeastern Asia to South America and Mexico, and from there to city streets and country roads in every nation. The cost of this trade runs into the billions of dollars. The people who manufacture, distribute, and possess heroin may, and often do, pay for their crimes with their freedom.

Traffic: The International Heroin Trade
All heroin in the United States comes from foreign sources and thus is brought to this country through

illegal smuggling. During the 1920s and 1930s, most heroin came from China. By the 1940s, countries in Southeast Asia (Laos, Thailand, and Burma, known as "The Golden Triangle") become the major market in the opium trade. Following World War II, European gangsters and their American counterparts of the Mafia controlled the heroin trade in the United States. During the early 1970s, the Mafia imported heroin from France, primarily from the city of Marseilles, where opium smuggled in from Turkey was refined and then sent to the United States. During the mid-1970s, heroin produced in Mexico—called Mexican brown—appeared. Today, the four regions of the world supplying heroin to the United States are South America, Southeast Asia (primarily Burma), Mexico, and southwestern Asia (primarily Afghanistan).

South America
Of the estimated six metric tons of heroin produced in Colombia during 1998, virtually all the heroin was believed to be destined for the U.S. market. The heroin trade in Colombia remains in the hands of numerous independent trafficking groups, and the drug is smuggled mainly in quantities of one to two kilograms by couriers aboard commercial airlines. The Dominican Republic also plays a significant role in heroin distribution in the United States, especially in East Coast cities such as New York, Baltimore, and Orlando. South

The Traffic and the Law

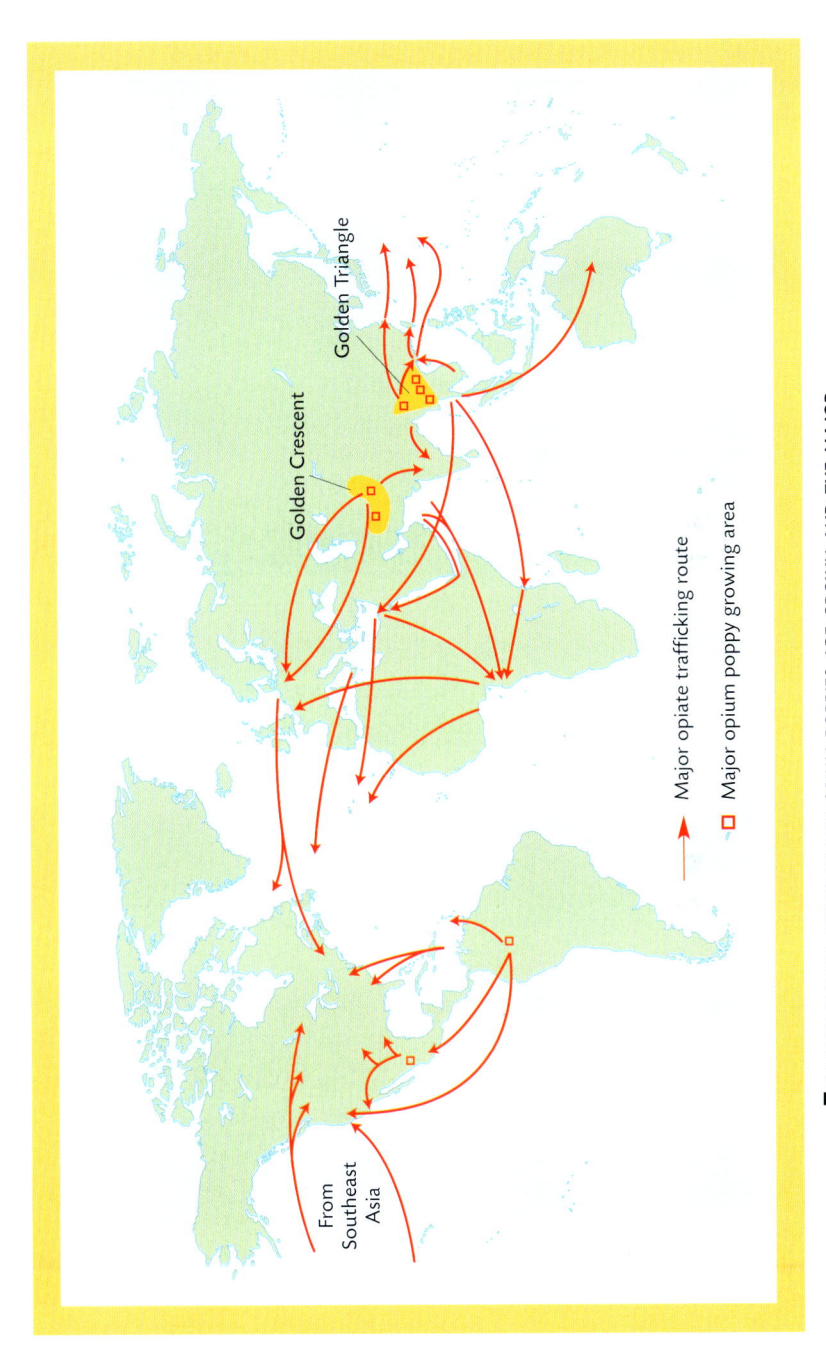

THIS MAP SHOWS AREAS WHERE OPIUM POPPIES ARE GROWN AND THE MAJOR TRAFFICKING ROUTES FROM PRODUCERS AROUND THE WORLD INTO THE UNITED STATES.

American heroin markets are also emerging in the District of Columbia, Atlanta, Miami, Fort Lauderdale, New Orleans, Detroit, and Chicago.

The flow of South American heroin began to increase dramatically in 1993, when Colombia-based drug organizations, already in control of the worldwide cocaine market, expanded into the heroin trade.

Southeast Asia
The so-called Golden Triangle, formed by the countries of Burma, Thailand, and Laos, remains the principal source of the world's opium. Opium produced in Burma flows largely overland through southern China to Hong Kong, Macau, and other regional commercial air and maritime centers. From there, couriers transport the drug to Australia, Taiwan, Europe, and North America by ship and by air. Another common route for Burmese heroin and opium is through Thailand, which moves overland through northern Thailand to Bangkok and southern Thailand for export. Laos, Vietnam, and Cambodia have emerged as secondary transit zones and markets for Burmese heroin and opium. While most Lao-produced heroin appears to be consumed domestically, Burmese heroin flows overland through Laos to China and Vietnam for local use and transshipment overseas.

Southeast Asian heroin and opium are smuggled to Australia from the Golden Triangle and China by commercial and noncommercial maritime means, as well as by couriers on scheduled flights. Most Southeast Asian heroin is imported into North America and western Europe in maritime containers, primarily via major shipping centers. Smaller amounts are brought to consuming nations by individual couriers on commercial flights.

Mexico

Although Mexico cultivates only about two percent of the world's opium, the vast majority of it is converted into heroin and smuggled directly into the United States by Mexican heroin trafficking organizations. Passenger bus routes along the western coast of Mexico towards Tijuana and other destinations along the Southwest border figure prominently in the shipments of loads of heroin. Major highway systems in Mexico also continue to provide a reliable system for transporting heroin to the United States. In addition, couriers move heroin through the airports in the United States and Mexican border cities.

Southwest Asia

Most Southwest Asian heroin flows overland through Iran and Turkey to Europe via the Balkans. Once in Turkey, smugglers use trucks, buses, or personal vehicles to transport heroin to western Europe for distribution throughout the rest of the world. Pakistan also exports heroin, largely by ship or

the facts about HEROIN

AN AFGHAN STREET TRADER SORTS THROUGH DRIED POPPY CAPSULES.

couriers on commercial air flights to the Middle East, Europe, Africa, Canada, and the United States. Since the fall of the Soviet Union, the Central Asian states, which include Turkmenistan, Uzbekistan, Tajikistan, Kazakhstan, and Kyrgyzstan, have emerged as important smuggling routes for southwest Asian heroin moving to or through Russia and eastern Europe.

The primary Southwest Asian source of heroin is Afghanistan. According to the United Nations Office on Drugs and Crime (UNODC), Afghanistan produced about 3,600 tons of opium in 2003, generating more than $2 billion of illicit income, a sum equivalent to more than 50 percent of the nation's legitimate gross domestic product. The drug trade in Afghanistan fosters instability and supports criminals, terrorists, and militias. Historic high prices now being commanded by opium are inhibiting the normal development of the Afghan economy by sidetracking the labor pool and diminishing the attractiveness of legal farming and economic activities. Most of the southwest Asian heroin, from Afghanistan and elsewhere, arrives in United States by couriers on commercial flights or by mail.

Methods of Transport
Traffickers transport heroin to the United States in three ways. Heavy foot and vehicle traffic at border crossings, particularly between the United States

Common Street Names for Heroin

Al Capone	Isda
Antifreeze	Jee gee
Ballot	Joy
Bart Simpson	Junk
Big bag	Lemonade
Big H	Mexican brown
Brown sugar	Nice and easy
Capital H	Noise
Cheese	Orgy
Chip	Old Steve
Crank	Orange line
Dead on Arrival	P-dope
Dirt	Pangonadalot
Dr. Feelgood	Peg
Ferry dust	Perfect high
George smack	Poison
Golden girl	Pure
Good horse	Rawhide
Hard candy	Ready rock
Hazel	Salt
Hero	Sweet dreams
Hombre	Train
Horse	White boy
HRN	Zoquete

and Mexico, facilitates the smuggling of heroin between countries and regions. Traffickers conceal shipments within commercial and private vehicles, or hide the drug on or in their body as they walk across the border. Trafficking groups use individual air couriers—sometimes called mules—to smuggle small amounts of heroin—1 to 2 kilograms—on commercial air flights. The mules hide the drug in their personal belongings or they ingest packets of heroin wrapped in plastic, a dangerous practice that leads to several deaths every year when the bags break or dissolve in the intestines, leaking large amounts of heroin into the body. Transporting heroin by ship or smaller vessels remains relatively rare, although it remains the principal method of transporting large amounts of Southeast Asian heroin.

Heroin Laws in the United States

The United States Congress first outlawed heroin in December 1914, when it passed the Harrison Narcotics Tax Act. This law called for control of each phase of the preparation and distribution of medicinal opium, morphine, heroin, cocaine, and any new derivatives of these substances. The act also criminalized the sale, purchase, and possession of these drugs. Heroin has been illegal in the United States ever since.

Now a twenty-four-year-old college student, Troy was arrested for possession of heroin when he was nineteen years old.

> *I know it sounds like a cliché, but it was the best thing that could have happened to me. I got probation along with drug court—where I have to go to court every week and get tested for drugs—and I have to attend meetings and other programs. But I was lucky. I know a lot of people who don't have lives now because they got caught dealing or didn't get a judge who cared enough to give them a second chance.*

Troy spent only three weeks in jail, while his family—cousins from out of state—raised money for his $10,000 bail.

> *In those three weeks, I learned a lot. I met a guy who was facing twenty years to life in prison because he already had been convicted three times of possession of cocaine and heroin. He never did anything violent, never even stole anything (at least not that he got caught for) but that's the law in my state. Four convictions and you're done.*

When Troy got out of jail, he was drug-free for the first time since he was twelve years old.

It wasn't that I couldn't have gotten some drugs in jail—there were drugs everywhere if you knew where to look—but I'd had enough. I was sick, I was tired, and—another cliché—I was sick and tired of being sick and tired. I'd gone through withdrawal in jail, and that was a nightmare. They only gave me some aspirin for the aches, nothing for the chills and the throwing up. It was awful.

Troy's experience in jail disturbed him so much that he made a decision that had eluded him for the seven years he'd been using drugs. "I knew, just knew, I didn't want to use anymore. It was a gut thing, not a head thing. I didn't think about it, I just did it. Every day is still a struggle, but I just picture that jail cell and I keep going forward."

Scheduling Drugs by Law

In 1970, the U.S. Congress passed the Controlled Substances Act. Through this act, drugs are placed into one of five "schedules," or categories. The U.S. Food and Drug Administration (FDA), with help from the DEA and medical experts, decide in which schedule a drug belongs based upon several categories: 1) the substance's medicinal value, 2) the substance's harmfulness, and 3) its potential for abuse or addiction. Schedule I is reserved for the most dangerous drugs that have no recognized medical use, while Schedule V is the classification used for the least dangerous drugs. The act also provides ways for new drugs to be added or removed from a schedule depending on new information about the drugs.

The factors that government officials use when deciding in which schedule a drug belongs include the following:

1. Its actual or relative potential for abuse.
2. Scientific evidence of its pharmacological effect, if known.
3. The state of current scientific knowledge regarding the drug or other substance.
4. Its history and current pattern of abuse.
5. The scope, duration, and significance of abuse.
6. What, if any, risk there is to the public health.

7. Its psychic or physiological dependence liability (however addictive it is).
8. Whether the substance is an immediate precursor (a chemical required for its manufacture) of a substance already controlled under this title.

Using these criteria, the FDA evaluates each new drug that comes into use—legally or illegally—and places it within one of five Schedules. In which Schedule a drug falls helps state and federal lawmakers decide what penalty a person convicted of possessing, manufacturing, or distributing the drug should receive.

Every state in the country enforces laws against possessing heroin. Possession of heroin in some states requires mandatory jail time—up to four years—even for a first-time offender. Those with prior convictions face even stiffer penalties. Those people arrested for distribution of heroin, or possession with intent to distribute the drug, may be charged at either the state or the federal level, and the sentences for these crimes are almost always mandatory. On the federal level, possession with intent to distribute heroin penalties range from a mandatory ten to twenty years in prison for first-time offenders. On the federal level, the DEA made a total of 2,329 heroin-related arrests during 2003, which represents about 8.6 percent of its total arrests.

the facts about HEROIN

It is important to note that not only is selling, buying, or possessing heroin a crime in the United States, but it also exacts other costs within the criminal justice system. Nearly 6 percent of males and 7 percent of females arrested for other crimes tested positive for opiates in 2003. There are a number of reasons why there is such a connection between using drugs and committing crimes. One factor, especially among young people, may be that committing crimes is another expression of the risk-taking behavior common to drug users. Another explanation is that most drug abusers are unable to support themselves and their habits by working in regular, legitimate jobs and therefore resort to crime.

PAST HEROIN USE BY ARRESTEE

THIS CHART SHOWS THE PERCENTAGE OF PEOPLE ARRESTED FOR VARIOUS CRIMES WHO ADMITTED TO HEROIN USE

DURATION OF USE	MALES	FEMALES
USED IN PAST 7 DAYS	3.3%	4.0%
USED IN PAST MONTH	3.9%	4.4%
USED IN PAST YEAR	5.1%	7.1%
AVERAGE NUMBER OF DAYS USED IN PAST MONTH	9.6 DAYS	9.9 DAYS

Source: National Institute of Justice, 2004

During the last two decades, the number of prisoners in state and federal institutions has grown from 200,000 to more than one million. More than 30 percent of the current state prison population and 60 percent of prisoners in federal custody are serving time for drug offenses, including those involving heroin possession, manufacture, and distribution.

The Thamkrabok Monastery in Thailand began treating opium addicts in the early 1960s. They have since become recognized worldwide for their drug detoxification programs.

5 Leaving Heroin Behind

ACCORDING TO a study conducted by Roper ASW, a prominent market research company for the Partnership for a Drug-Free America, the percentage of teens who have seen or heard anti-drug ads during the past five years has increased by 63 percent. The number of teens who have "learned a lot" about the risks of drug use from these ads has increased about 65 percent, which means the message is getting through.

Most teens now know how dangerous heroin is. Asked what the risks of heroin use are, students said: "heroin can wreck your life"; "heroin is a dangerously addictive drug"; "heroin is not a glamorous, cool drug." According to the Roper ASW poll, about one in seven teens (16 percent) reported having close friends who have tried heroin. Only about 4 percent of teens have ever tried heroin.

That's the good news. The bad news is that there are an estimated one million heroin addicts living in the United States today. Many of them are teenagers, and many more of them began using heroin in their teen years. For those people, young and old, quitting the habit of heroin is the only safe way to move forward with their lives.

Treating Heroin Addiction

Heroin is a highly addictive substance. The drug causes changes in the brain that trigger constant and severe psychological and physical cravings for the drug. Breaking an addiction to heroin, therefore, means finding other ways to satisfy the craving long enough for addicts to try to solve the problems in their lives instead of escaping them through drug use. These problems may have prompted drug use in the first place or they may have developed as a result of the addiction.

The first step in the process of breaking heroin addiction is physical withdrawal from the drug. One way to do this is to quit "cold turkey"—or withdraw from heroin all at once and without using other medications to treat the short- and long-term withdrawal symptoms that occur. The first eight to twenty-four hours of going cold turkey are the toughest because the body reacts violently to the withdrawal of the drug. Once a person quitting heroin makes it through this period, there will be fewer side effects related to withdrawal and, if he or she learns to cope with the social and familial problems that may underlie or stem from the addiction, it will get easier to resist taking the drug again.

Using heroin wreaks havoc in users' personal, professional, and social lives. Programs designed to treat these issues are now quite common. Today, psychological counseling, self-help groups, residential programs, and even medication are widely available to help heroin addicts of all ages.

Most heroin addicts experience overwhelming feelings of guilt and shame about the way they behaved while taking the drug. Most addicted individuals feel shame because drug-using behavior often conflicts with their own values and morals. Ironically, using heroin becomes a way to avoid facing the truth about their behavior and thus dealing with their emotions. An experienced counselor, another recovering addict, or trusted clergy can be of great help. Most good treatment programs have these people on staff.

It is important to note that it takes some people several attempts at kicking the habit—and many stays at treatment centers—before they succeed. This difficulty speaks to the power of the drug to alter mood and brain chemistry so that the craving for it overwhelms the best intentions. Fortunately, there are support groups and even medication that help bolster and enhance the success of behavioral and other psychological therapies.

Self-Help Programs

Organizations, treatment centers, and hotlines to help people quit using heroin, alcohol, and other drugs exist throughout the United States. Some programs require people to remain at the center as inpatients while others provide outpatient counseling, which means that members attend scheduled therapy sessions but live at home.

Among the resources available are what are known as twelve-step programs. Participating heroin abusers battle their addiction in part by learning from and helping other recovering addicts realize that there is life after heroin. These programs include Narcotics Anonymous and Alcoholics Anonymous, among others. According to the Narcotics Anonymous Web site, the goals of the program include:

- seeking help
- engaging in a thorough self-examination
- confidential self-disclosure
- making amends for harm done
- helping other drug addicts who want to recover.

Like other twelve-step programs, Narcotics Anonymous requires addicts to meet regularly in order to discuss their challenges and share their successes. One of the most widely-recognized characteristics of twelve-step groups is the requirement that members admit that they are indeed addicted and have no control over their use of the drug. Members share their experiences and provide peer support for each other. Many people who have joined these groups report they found success that previously eluded them, while others, including some ex-members, criticize their methods.

Successful recovery programs strongly urge that heroin addicts kicking the habit attend daily meetings for at least the first ninety days of sobriety. Individuals who successfully abstain from heroin generally attend many twelve-step meetings for support and accountability. They often report that a part of them still tries to justify using heroin. Daily meetings remind them of their powerlessness over drugs.

Counseling and Behavioral Therapy
Many behavioral treatments have been found to be effective for heroin addiction, including both residential and outpatient approaches. After an abuser's physical condition is under control, treatment for the underlying addiction may begin. This treatment may occur in either an inpatient setting (at a hospital or drug rehabilitation center) or through an outpatient program. Recovery begins and continues with a learning process of breaking old habits, severing ties with drug using friends, and identifying and then avoiding "triggers" that increase the desire to use heroin.

A CHEMICAL DEPENDENCE SUPPORT GROUP. THERAPY IS PART OF MOST SUCCESSFUL DRUG TREATMENT PROGRAMS.

Another psycho-social intervention is called cognitive-behavioral therapy. Such treatment is a short-term, focused approach to helping addicted individuals to abstain from heroin and other substances. The underlying assumption is that learning processes play an important role in the development and continuation of drug abuse and dependence. A therapist helps recovering addicts use the same learning processes to reduce their drug use. This approach attempts to help addicts recognize the situations in which they are most likely to use heroin, avoid these situations when appropriate, and cope more effectively with a range of problems and behaviors associated with drug abuse. As is true with behavioral strategies, therapists encourage patients to identify these triggers and to restructure their lifestyles to avoid them.

In addition to twelve-step programs and individual and group therapies, there are medical interventions available to treat heroin addiction. One such treatment is methadone therapy, which has been used for decades to help wean addicts from the drug. Two relatively new medications, naltrexone and buprenorphine, work in different ways to help those recovering from heroin addiction.

Methadone: Substitute for Heroin

Every day, an estimated 15,000 Americans take the prescribed medication methadone or its longer-acting cousin, LAAM (levo-alpha-acetyl-methadol). Methadone and LAAM are synthetic opiates used as maintenance treatment for heroin addiction. Studies find that two-thirds of methadone patients eventually stop using heroin and start improving their lives.

Taken orally once a day, methadone suppresses heroin withdrawal symptoms for between twenty-four and thirty-six hours, while LAAM stays effective for about seventy-two hours. Both drugs reduce the cravings associated with heroin use and block the high from heroin. Although chemically similar to heroin, methadone differs in several important ways. First, because users take it orally, they do not experience the "rush" that comes from injecting or snorting the drug. Also, it is long-acting, so that the patient no longer experiences the ups and

the facts about HEROIN

A METHADONE LAB. FOR MORE THAN THIRTY YEARS THIS SYNTHETIC NARCOTIC HAS BEEN USED TO TREAT OPIOID ADDICTION.

downs that accompany the waxing and waning of heroin levels in the blood for a day or two. Furthermore, methadone actually blocks the high that comes from heroin use so that a patient taking methadone has little motivation to use heroin again. Although the patient is physically dependent on the drug, he or she does not experience the same compulsive and disruptive use of the drug seen with heroin addiction.

Research also indicates that long-term treatment with methadone is safe. If administered under medical supervision, methadone does not cause any damage to the body nor does it have any serious side effects. Treatment with methadone improves former addicts' lives, as well as the life of the communities in which they live. National Institute on Drug Abuse statistics show that criminal activity among former heroin users who were now methadone patients decreased by more than 53 percent and full-time employment grew by 24 percent.

Buprenorphine: Relief from Withdrawal
Like methadone, buprenorphine is a medication designed to relieve withdrawal symptoms in heroin addicts trying to kick their habit. Buprenorphine is less powerful than methadone but is considered to be less addictive and perhaps safer, making it especially attractive for patients who are mildly or moderately addicted.

A tablet form of buprenorphine is already in use in the United States and around the world as a once-daily treatment for opioid dependence. An injectable form of the drug, designed to relieve symptoms for much longer per dose than the tablet form, is currently under investigation.

One study, funded by the National Institute on Drug Abuse (NIDA), found that a single injection of a sustained-release formulation of buprenorphine effectively relieved withdrawal symptoms for six weeks in heroin-dependent patients. The NIDA

DR. WARREN BICKEL (RIGHT) OF THE UNIVERSITY OF VERMONT. BICKEL WAS THE LEAD PHYSICIAN IN RESEARCHING BUPRENORPHINE, AN OPIATE WITHDRAWAL DRUG.

research team, led by Dr. George Bigelow at Johns Hopkins University School of Medicine, administered the buprenorphine injection to five addicted heroin users. During four weeks of residential treatment and two weeks of outpatient treatment, the scientists assessed patients for signs and symptoms of heroin withdrawal. The patients also received weekly injections of the opioid hydromorphone dilaudid to test whether their sensitivity to this class of opioids was reduced by the buprenorphine treatment. The researchers found that a single dose of the sustained-release form of buprenorphine provided relief of withdrawal symptoms and reduced the effects of the test opioid for six weeks.

The findings from the current study, the first to test this new formulation of buprenorphine in humans, may lead to more treatment options for individuals addicted to heroin. A long-acting form of buprenorphine may increase patient adherence to treatment, ease the burden of visits to treatment providers, make treatment more accessible, and reduce the risk of buprenorphine misuse.

Both forms of buprenorphine fall under Schedule III of the Controlled Substances Act, which places them on par with drugs like Tylenol with Codeine in terms of potential for abuse and illegal diversion. According to the FDA, buprenorphine is considered to have less risk for causing psychological and or physical dependence than the drugs in Schedule II, such as morphine, OxyContin, or methadone.

Naltrexone: Turning Off the Switch
First used as a treatment to support people who quit using alcohol after becoming dependent, naltrexone is now prescribed to help people maintain abstinence after they have withdrawn from heroin.

Naltrexone is what is known as an "opioid antagonist." It works by blocking the opioid receptors in the brain and therefore blocking the effects of heroin. Doctors hope that if addicts taking naltrexone know that they cannot achieve a high from using heroin, they will be better able to resist using it. However, the drug does nothing to stop the physical or psychological dependency on heroin. Fortunately, naltrexone is not addictive nor does it produce any euphoric effects.

To be eligible for naltrexone treatment, addicts must be free of heroin and other opioids for seven to ten days and be highly motivated to break their addiction. People trying naltrexone treatment who have support from family or friends are more likely to benefit from the treatment.

The greatest risk associated with naltrexone is when heroin is used either after a naltrexone dose has been skipped or if a person stops taking naltrexone altogether. While the person is on naltrexone, tolerance to heroin decreases. Therefore, if a recovering addict uses heroin, the risk of overdosing from heroin is greatly increased. Overdose may occur if the person uses the same or even a smaller amount of heroin compared to what they used before being on naltrexone.

Staying Drug Free

Before addicts can begin any form of drug treatment, it's important that they learn about their treatment options from a qualified health professional. Such information includes the length of the program, how much it costs, what other supports are included or recommended, all the risks and side effects, and any other health issues to consider.

For heroin users and addicts, the benefits of kicking the heroin habit are great. Staying off heroin can provide the opportunity to experience life to its fullest, including developing more close and stable relationships with loved ones, learning and growing at school or college, and achieving financial and career success.

GLOSSARY

addiction: A pattern of behavior based on great physical and/or psychological need for a substance or activity.

anxiety: Uneasiness, worry, uncertainty, and fear that come with thinking about an anticipated danger.

central nervous system (CNS): The nerve cells making up the brain and spinal cord.

codeine: A substance found in opium and used as a painkiller in cough syrups and other prescription medicines.

dopamine: A neurotransmitter, or chemical messenger, in the brain. The chemicals in heroin affect the amount and action of dopamine.

dynorphin: A neurotransmitter that is affected by opiates such as heroin.

endorphin: A neurotransmitter that helps to elevate mood and alleviate pain.

morphine: A naturally occurring substance found in the opium poppy that acts as a powerful narcotic painkiller when ingested.

narcotic: A drug that induces drowsiness and stupor. Morphine and other morphine-like compounds, including heroin, are narcotics.

neurons: Nerve cells, the basic units of the nervous system.

neurotransmitters: Chemicals in the brain (including dopamine and dynorphin) that act to send nerve signals. Neurotransmitters are released by neurons. When an imbalance among the neurotransmitters occurs, emotional and physical symptoms result.

opiate: One of a group of drugs derived from opium, which is an extract of the poppy plant that depresses brain function.

opioid: Synthetic drugs that behave like opiates; they are not derived from opium.

Papaver somniferum: A summer-flowering annual plant of the poppy family grown in hot, dry climates for the drug opium, which is extracted from its sap. The raw material is refined to produce heroin.

synapse: The gap between the nerve endings of two neurons.

tolerance: A condition in which a drug user needs increasing amounts of a drug to achieve the same level of intoxication once obtained from using smaller amounts.

withdrawal: A condition resulting from stopping the use of a drug. Symptoms of withdrawal from heroin may include intense physical and psychological cravings, fatigue, sweating, cramps, chills, diarrhea, nausea, depression, and anxiety.

FURTHER INFORMATION

Books

Ashton, Robert. *This is Heroin*. London: Sanctuary Publishing Ltd., 2002.

Godfrey, Martin. *Understanding Drugs: Heroin*. New York: Franklin Watts, 1987.

Kuhn, Cynthia, Ph.D., Scott Swartzwelder, and Wilkie Wilson. *Buzzed: The Straight Facts About the Most Used and Abused Drugs from Alcohol to Ecstasy*. New York: W. W. Norton & Company, 2003.

Kuhn, Cynthia, Scott Swartzwelder, and Wilkie Wilson. *Just Say Know: Talking with Kids about Drugs and Alcohol*. New York:

W. W. Norton &r Company, 2002.
Medical Surveys
Centers for Disease Control and Prevention. *Youth Risk Behavior Surveillance–United States, 2003*, May 2004.

National Institute on Drug Abuse and University of Michigan. *Monitoring the Future National Survey Results on Drug Use, 1975-2003*, 2004.

U.S. Sentencing Commission. *2002 Sourcebook of Federal Sentencing Statistics*, 2004.

Web Sites
Alateen
www.al-anon.org

Partnership for a Drug Free America
www.drugfreeameria.org

National Institute on Drug Abuse
www.nida.nig.gov/

Neuroscience for Kids
http://faculty.washington.edu/chudler/neurok.html

Office of National Drug Control Policy
www.whitehousedrugpolicy.gov

INDEX

Page numbers in **boldface** are illustrations and tables.

acetic anhydride, 12, 19
acquired immunodeficiency syndrome (AIDS), **21**, 23, **23**, 44, **46**
addiction, 12, 13
  basic components of, 53, 56-57
  cost of, 8, 15
  health risks, 39, 48-49
  scheduling drugs and, 70, 71
  treating, 76-86
addictive substances, 14-15, 22
additives, 19, 21, 43
Afghanistan, **58**, 60, **64**, 65
alcohol, 15, 49, 53, 78, 86
  in heroin combination, 21, 37, 52, 54
Alcoholics Anonymous, 49, 78
Alexander the Great, 10
amphetamines, 37-38
analgesics, 31
anesthetic, 39
anti-drug ads, 75
anxiety, 47, 50-52, 51
Arrestee-Drug Abuse Monitoring Program, 23-24
arthritis, **23**
axon, 28, **29**, 30, **30**

barbiturates, 37, 54
Bayer pharmaceutical laboratories, 13, **14**
behavioral therapy, 79, 80
Belushi, John, 39
Bickel, Warren, **84**
Bigelow, George, 85
black tar heroin, 18
blood-brain barrier, 20, 22
brain
  anatomy of, 27-28, 50-51
  biochemical processes, 28, 30-32
  blood-brain barrier, 20, 22
  heroin effect on, 20, **26**, 27, 35-36, 42, 47, 50-51, 53, 76-77
British East India Company, 12
buprenorphine, 81, 83-85, **84**
Burma, 60, 62

cancer, 33, 47
cell body, 28, **29**
Centers for Disease Control and Prevention, **44**
central nervous system (CNS), 22, **26**, 37, 39
cerebral cortex, 28
"chasing the dragon", 35
children of abusers, 42
China, 10, 12, 62

Index

"China White", 33
cirrhosis, 47
"club drug", 39
Cobain, Kurt, 55, **55**
cocaine, 38, 48, 62, 67, 68
  in heroin combination, 21, 37, 39, 45, 52
codeine, 32, 85
cognitive-behavioral therapy, 79-81, **80**
"cold turkey", 76
Colombia, 60
Controlled Substances Act, 70
  scheduled drugs, 70, 71, 85
cough suppressant, 10, 13, **14**, 32
counseling, 78, 79-81
courier transport, 60, 62-65, 67
crime, drug use and, 23, 24, 72

death, risk of, 20-21, 32-33, 52
  heroin combination, 37, 39, 47
Demerol, 33
dendrite, 28, **29**, 30
dependence, development of, 21-22, 53, 56
depressant, 37, 39
  heroin as, 20, **23**, 47, 50-51
depression, clinical, 42, 47, 50
diazepam, 52
Dilaudid, 85
distribution, penalties for, 71-73
dopamine, 27, 32
Dreser, Heinrich, 13
Drug and Alcohol Dependence, 45
"drug court", 49, 68
drug detoxification program, **74**
dynorphin, 31

Ecstasy, 39
emotion, 28, 41, 77
endogenous opioids, 31
endorphin, 27, 31
enkephalins, 31
euphoria, 23, 32, 35, **40**, 86

Farndon, Pete, 54
"fear-alarm" system, 51
fentanyl, 33

Galen, 10
gamma hydroxy butyrate (GHB), 39
Golden Crescent, **61**
Golden Triangle, 60, **61**, 62

hallucinogenic drugs, 39
Harrison Narcotics Tax Act, 14, 67
Hendrix, Jimi, 54
hepatitis, 34, 43, 45
  hepatitis B, 23, **23**
  hepatitis C (HCV), **21**, 23, **23**, 45-47, 48-49
heroin, 7-8, 33
  as addictive, 7, 14-15, 22, **23**, 36, 38
  additives, 19, 21, 43
  in combination, 21, 37-39, 45, 47, 52, 54
  common street names, 66
  creation of, 12-13, 15-19
  effects of, 23, 23, 41-42
  effects on brain, 28, 31, 32, 36, 39, 42
  experience of, 36-37
  history of, 8-15, **9**, **11**, **13**, **14**
  as legal problem, 23-25, 39, 42, 49, 57, 67, 68-69
  as medical problem, 20-22, 23, 25, 39, 42-43, 48-49, 56-57
  purity/potency, 19, 21, 36, 43, 47
  raw materials for, **6**, 7-8, 15-16, **16**
  risk, 19-23, 25, 37, 75
  as social problem, 17, 22-25, 38-39, 48, 56, 76
  types of, **18**, 34
  use today, 24
  ways of using, 20-22, 34-36
  withdrawal symptoms, 50-53, **51**
heroin laws, 67
"high", 31, 36-37, 48, 81, 83, 86
Hippocrates, **9**, 10
von Hohenheim, Bombast, 11
Holiday, Billie, 54
Honeyman-Scott, James, 54

Hul Gil (joy plant), 8
human immunodeficiency virus (HIV), **23**, 34, 43-45, 49

illicit drug use, 7, 23-24, 47, 59, 67
immediate precursor, 71
injection of heroin, 17, 19, **21**, 34-39, **40**, 48-49, 81
  intramuscular, 20, 34
  intravenous, 20, 34, 35, **46**
  risk, 22-23, 43, **44**, 45-47, **46**
injection of opiate analogs, 33

Joplin, Janis, 54

laudanum, 11, 12, **13**
levo-alpha-acetyl-methadol (LAAM), 81
lifestyles, 80-81
liver disease, 23, **23**, 47, 49
locus coeruleus, 50, 51
LSD, 39

Mafia, 60
marijuana (pot), 15, 48
MDMA, 39
medical intervention, 77, 81-86
medicinal use, 67, 70
  historic use of opium, 10, 12-14, **13**, 32
  of opiate analogs, 33
meditation, 10
Melvoin, Jonathan, 55
mental health issues, 42
meperidine, 33-34
methadone, 52, 81, **82**, 83, 85
Mexican brown, 60, 66
Mexico, 60, 63, 67
Monitoring the Future study, 24, 25
mood disorders, 47-50
Morpheus, 11
morphine, 11-14, 13, 19, 32-33, 67, 85
  raw material for, 6, 8, 11, 18
  withdrawal, 50-52, **51**
MPTP, 34
mules, 67

naltrexone, 81, 86
narcotics, 8, 10, 14-15
Narcotics Anonymous (NarcAnon), 49, 78
National Institute on Drug Abuse (NIDA), 33, 83, 84-85
National Institutes of Health, 45, 47
nausea symptom, 17, 20, **23**, 32, 36-38, 51
needle sharing, 43, **44**, 45, 46
neurons, 28, **29**, 30, **30**, 53
neurotransmitters, 27, 30, **30**, 31-32, 53
"new heroin", 34
nicotine, 53
No. 3 heroin, 19
No. 4 heroin, 19

"on the nod", 35, **40**
opiate analogs, 32-34
opiates, 22, 26, 27-28, 31-32, 50-52, 84
  heroin as, 22, 37
  synthetic, 81, 82
opioid antagonist, 86
opioid drugs, 14, 20-21, 31-32, **82**, 84-86
opium dens, 10-11, 12
opium gum, 15, 16, **16**, 19
opium poppy, **6**, 7, 8, 61, 67
  harvest process, 8, 16, **16**
  historic use of, 10-14, 13, 32
  life cycle of, 15
  refining process, 19
opium trade, 10-12, 60, 63, 65
Opium War, 12
outpatient programs, 78, 79, 85
overdose, 33, 50, 52, 54-55, 86
  heroin combination and, 37, 39
  opiate analogs and, 33
  swallowing risk, 35, 43
oxycodone, 33, 52
OxyContin, 85

pain-relieving medication, 7, **9**, 10-12, **13**, **23**, 31-34
Papaver somniferum, 8, 15

Index

Paracelsus, 11
Parkinson's disease, 34
Partners for a Drug-Free America, 75
peer support, 79
Percodan, 33
Pfaff, Kristin, 55
Phoenix, River, 39
physical dependency, 22, 76, 85, 86
"pleasure system", **26**, 27, 32
possession penalties, 71, 72, 73
possession with intent to distribute penalties, 71, 72
prison statistics, 73
psychological counseling, 77, 78
psychological dependency, 22, 56, 76-77, 85-86
Pure Food and Drug Act, 14

receptor molecules, 20, 30-32, 86
recovering addicts, risks for, 50
recreational drug use, **11**, 38
residential programs, 77, 78-79, 85
respiration, effects on, 20, **23**, 32, 33, 37, 42, 47
Roper ASW poll, 75
"runner high", 31
"rush", 20, **23**, 36, 41, 81

scheduling drugs, 70-73, 85
sedatives, 39
self-help groups, 77, 78-79
Serturner, Wilhelm, 11
sex risks, 38, 45
"skin pop", 35
slow-down function, 20, 21
smoking drugs, 15, 19, 20, 35, 36
smuggling, 60, 65, 67
snorting drugs, 17, 20, 33-34, 36, 38, 48, 81
South America, 60, **61**, 62
Southeast Asia, 60, **61**, 62-63, 67
Southwest Asia, **58**, 60, **61**, 63, **64**, 65
"speedball", 39, 54
spinal cord, **26**
Spungen, Nancy, 54
stimulants, 37, 39, 48

stress, opiates and, 31, 42
student usage, 24, **24**, 25, 76
  anti-drug message and, 75, 76
  risky behavior and, 38, 41, 72
styptic usage, 10
suicide, 50, 55
swallowing drugs, 20, 33, 35
synapse, 28, **29**, 30, **30**

Thamrabok Monastery, **74**
Thunders, Johnny, 54
tolerance, 21-22, 32, 53, 56, 86
trafficking internationally, 8, 10, **58**, 59-67
  major routes, **61**
  method of transport, 65, 67
tranquilizers, 37
treatment, 38, **74**, 76-78, 87
  types of, 78-81, **82**, 83-86
"triggers", 28, 79, 81
tuberculosis, 13, 32
twelve-step program, 49, 78-79, 81
Tylenol, 85

United Nations International Drug Control Program (UNDCP), 7
United Nations Office on Drugs and Crime (UNODC), 65
U.S. Civil War, 12, **13**
U.S. Drug Enforcement Administration (DEA), 23, 70, 71, **72**
U.S. Food and Drug Administration (FDA), 70, 71, 85
U.S. National Survey on Drug Use and Health, 7-8

Valium, 52
Vicious, Sid, 54
vomiting center, 32, 36
vomiting symptoms, 20, **23**, 32, 36, 50, 69

withdrawal, 22, 34, 49, 76, **84**
  side effects, 77, 83
  symptoms, 22, 37, 50-53, **51**, 57, 69, 76-77, 81, 83-85
women, heroin risk for, **23**, 42

ABOUT THE AUTHOR

Suzanne Levert is the author of more than twenty-five young adult and adult nonfiction titles. She specializes in health and medical subjects as well as the social sciences. Ms. Levert has written five books in the Marshall Cavendish Benchmark *Drugs* series. Born in Natick, Massachusetts, Ms. Levert now practices law in New Orleans, Louisiana, where she comes face to face with the legal and social problems caused by illegal drug addiction and trafficking.